Our Bodies

Our Blood

Charlotte Guillain

Heinemann Library
Chicago, Illinois

www.heinemannraintree.com
Visit our website to find out more information about Heinemann-Raintree books.

To order:

☎ Phone 888-454-2279

🖥 Visit www.heinemannraintree.com to browse our catalog and order online.

Editorial: Rebecca Rissman, Laura Knowles, Nancy Dickmann, and Sian Smith
Picture research: Ruth Blair and Mica Brancic
Designed by Joanna Hinton-Malivoire
Original Illustrations © Capstone Global Library Ltd. 2010
Illustrated by Tony Wilson
Printed and bound by Leo Paper Group

14 13 12 11 10
10 9 8 7 6 5 4 3 2 1

Library of Congress Cataloging-in-Publication Data

Guillain, Charlotte.
  Our blood / Charlotte Guillain.
    p. cm. -- (Our bodies)
  Includes bibliographical references and index.
  ISBN 978-1-4329-3595-5 (hc) -- ISBN 978-1-4329-3604-4 (pb)
1. Blood--Juvenile literature. I. Title.
QP91.G896 2010
612.1'1--dc22
                          2009022299

Acknowledgments
The author and publisher are grateful to the following for permission to reproduce copyright material: Alamy pp.**9** (© INSADCO Photography), **11** (© shockpix.com), **13** (© Jochen Tack); Corbis pp.**4** (©Mark A. Johnson), **5** (©John-Francis Bourke/zefa), **22** (©Mark A. Johnson); iStockphoto pp.**8**, **16**, **17**, **23** (© Francisco Romero), **18** (© Terry J Alcorn), **20** (© Rob Friedman); Photolibrary p.**21**; Science Photo Library pp.**10** (Susumu Nishinaga), **19**, **23** (© Dr P. Marazzi).

Front cover photograph of a child with scraped knee reproduced with permission of iStockphoto (© Carmen Martínez Banús). Back cover photograph reproduced with permission of iStockphoto (© Terry J Alcorn).

Every effort has been made to contact copyright holders of any material reproduced in this book. Any omissions will be rectified in subsequent printings if notice is given to the publisher.

Contents

Body Parts

Our bodies have many parts.

head

arm

leg

hand

foot

Our bodies have parts on
the outside.

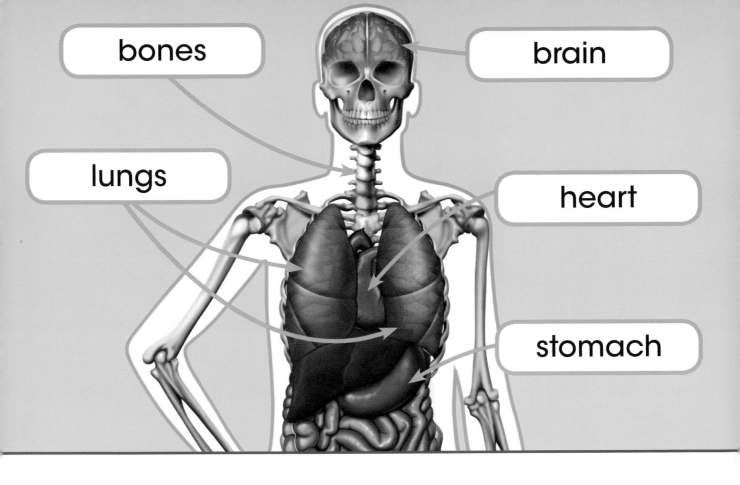

bones

brain

lungs

heart

stomach

Our bodies have parts on the inside.

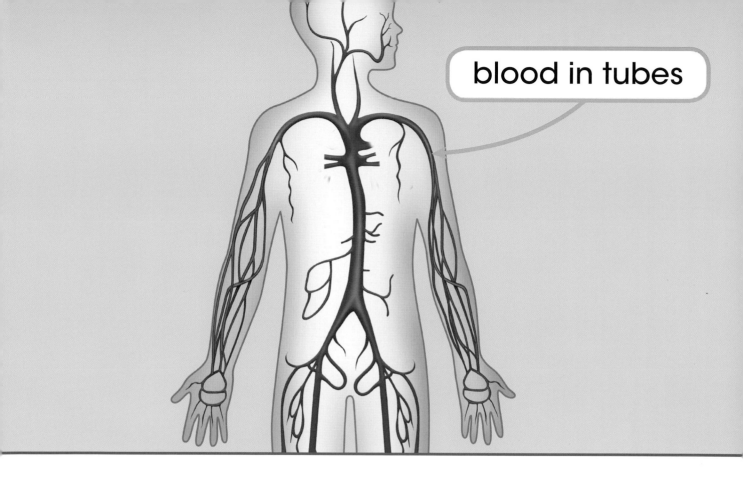

Your blood is inside your body.

Your Blood

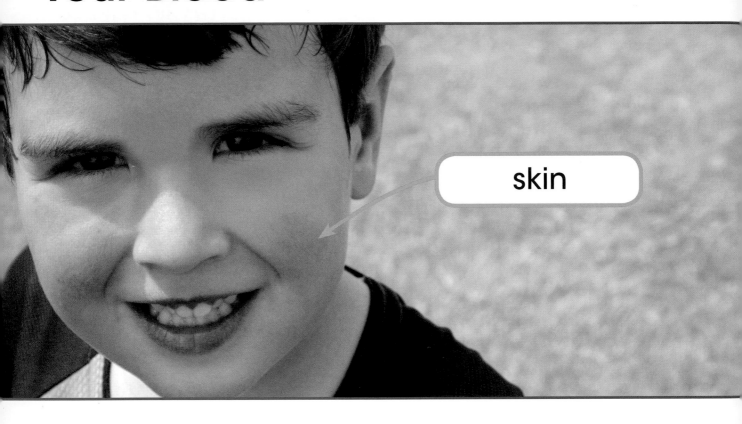

skin

Your blood is under your skin.

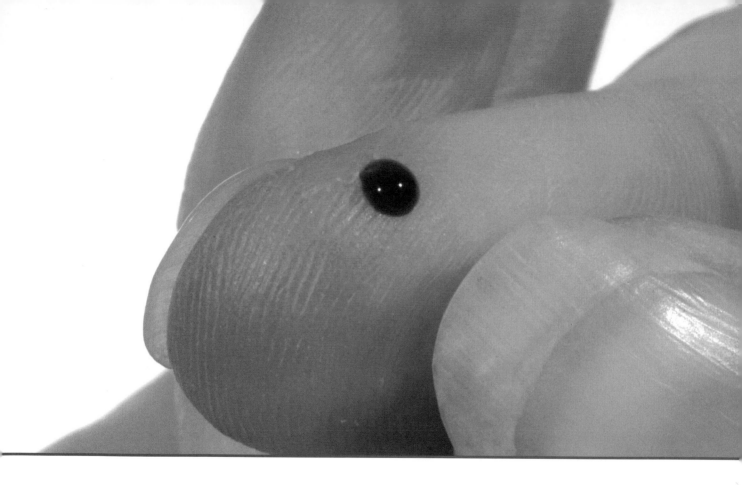

You can see some of your blood if
you get a cut.

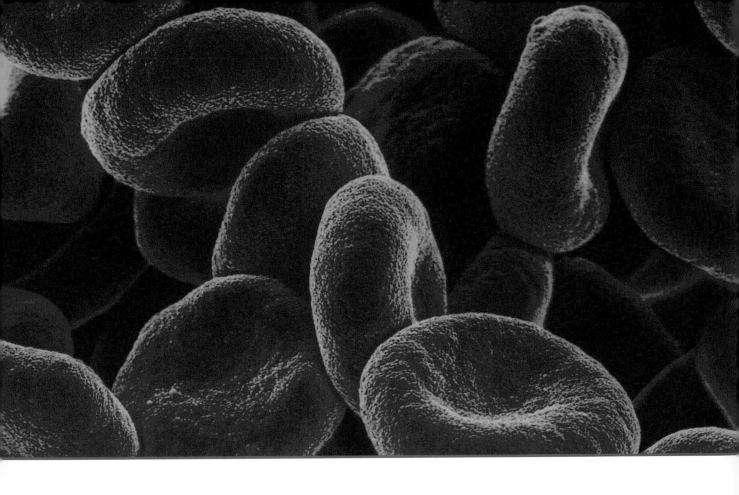

Blood is red.

Blood is wet.

Moving Blood

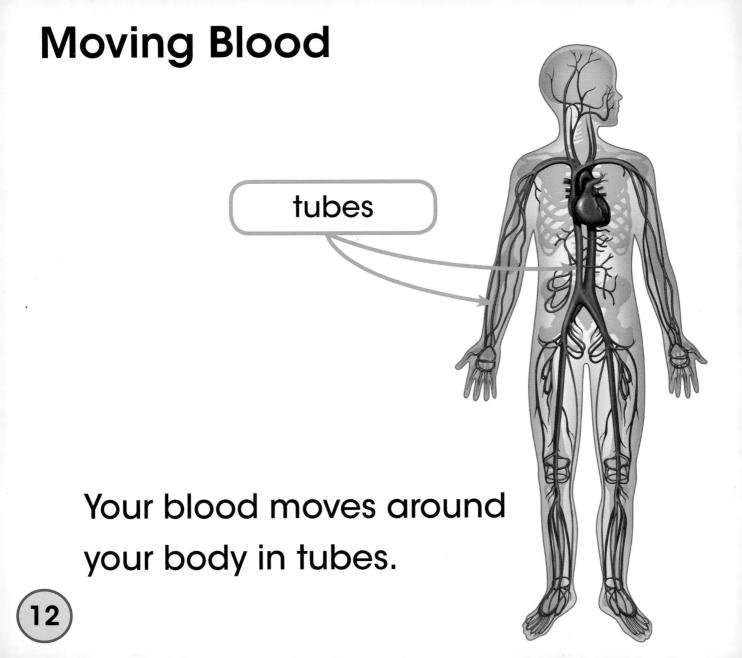

tubes

Your blood moves around your body in tubes.

Sometimes you can feel your
blood moving.

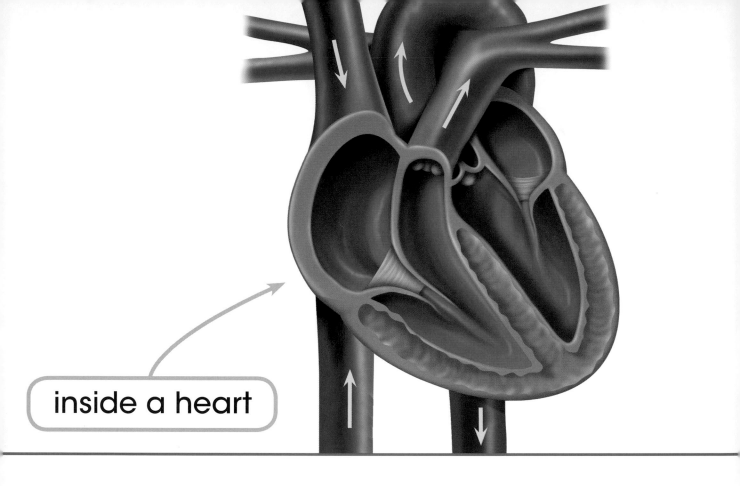

inside a heart

Your heart pushes blood around your body.

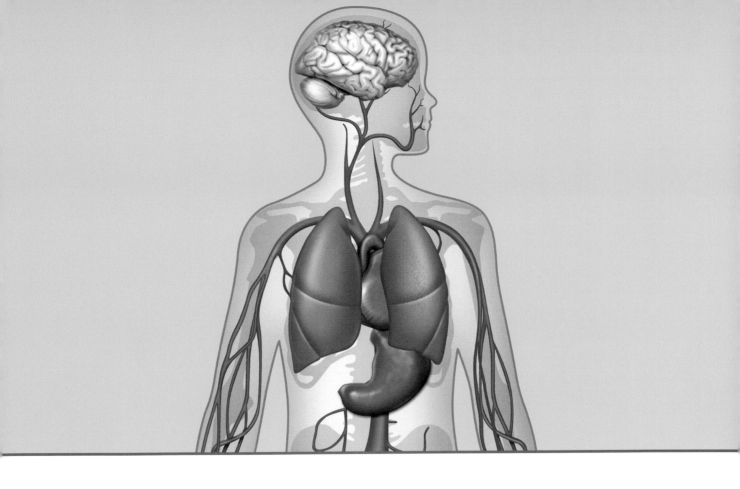

Your blood moves to all your
body parts.

What Does Blood Do?

Your blood carries food to your body parts.

Your blood carries air to your
body parts.

Your blood helps to keep your body parts warm or cool.

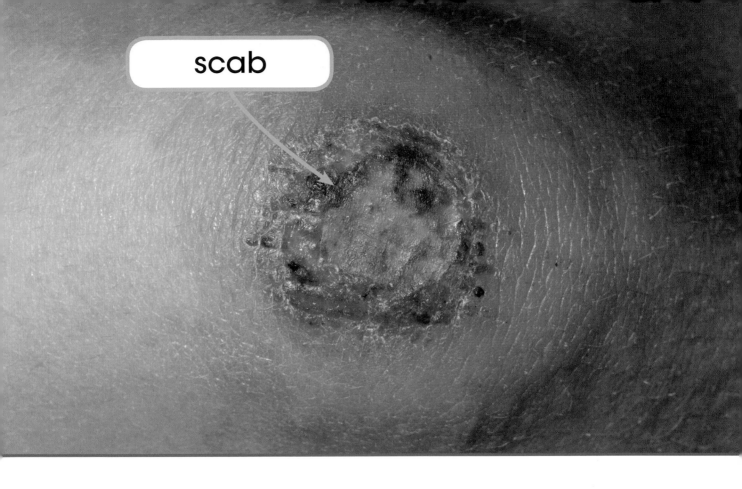

scab

Your blood can heal a cut on your skin.

Staying Healthy

You can drink water to help your blood.

You can eat healthy food to help your blood.

Quiz

Where in your body is your blood?

Answer on page 24

Picture Glossary

 **air** we need to breathe air in to stay alive. Air is all around us but we cannot see it.

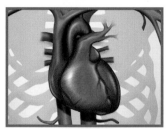 **heart** part of your body inside your chest. Your heart pushes blood around your body.

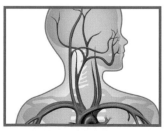 **scab** something your body makes to cover up a cut on your skin. New skin starts to grow under the scab.

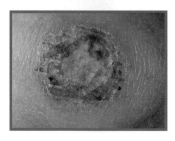 **tube** a long, thin pipe like a hose. Things can move through tubes because they have an empty space in the middle.

Index

Answer to quiz on page 22: Your blood is in all your body parts.

Notes to parents and teachers

Before reading

Ask children to name the parts of their body they can see on the outside. Then ask them what parts of their body are inside. Make a list of them together and see if the children know what each body part does, for example, stomachs break down food. Discuss where their blood is and ask it anyone knows what blood is for.

After reading

• Ask children to look at one another's faces and observe how they look. Then ask them to feel their own faces and observe the temperature. Then take the children outside and tell them to run around for five minutes. When they stop, ask them to look at each other's faces: What do they notice? What else makes our faces turn red and hot? What is happening?